Extra Credit

The 7 Things Every College Student
Needs to Know About Credit, Debt & Ca$h

By Bill Pratt, MBA

Author of The Graduate's Guide to Life and Money

Published by
Viaticus Publishing
4104 Sterling Trace Dr
Winterville NC 28590 U.S.A.

www.ExtraCreditBook.com

ISBN: 978-0-9818702-1-2

Printed in U.S.A.

Viaticus Pulishing.
    Extra Credit: The 7 things every college student needs to
know about credit, debt & ca$h, 2E/ by Bill Pratt.
    ISBN: 978-0-9818702-1-2

This publication is designed to provide accurate and authoritative
information with regard to the subject matter covered. It is sold
with the understanding that the publisher is not engaged in
rendering legal, accounting, or other professional advice. Since
individual situations may be fact dependent, and if expert advice
is required, the services of a competent professional should be
sought.

This book is available at quantity discounts for bulk purchases.
For information visit www.inceptia.org/books.

Contents

Foreword

Going to college helps you have a better life. As the president of an organization that helps college students achieve the dream of a higher education, I've seen first-hand how college can improve lives. It's a powerful investment in your future. I've also seen the devastation that students experience when they borrow too much or they don't learn money management skills they need to avoid financial mistakes while they're in college. Your *financial* education is just as important as your education in science, the arts, in business or any other field you choose. *Extra Credit: The 7 Things Every College Student Needs to Know About Credit, Debt and Ca$h* will help get your financial education started.

Bill Pratt shares my passion for teaching college students to succeed financially, not just while they're in college, but for the rest of their lives. As a former credit card company executive, Bill saw how financial mistakes can ruin lives. He left the for-profit world to teach full-time at East Carolina University, where he's helping create a robust personal finance program for college students to address their unique needs. He wrote *Extra Credit* to give college students a handy, easy-to-read reference for managing money and staying out of financial trouble.

If you are a new college student (or the parent of one) who needs practical advice about avoiding the financial pitfalls you'll face in college (like staring down credit card offers, dodging debit card fees, or choosing the best student loan, for instance), then *Extra Credit* will give you a mega-dose of information that's easy to understand. There are no complicated theories or difficult algorithms, just straightforward counsel you can actually use.

Completing college will help you have a better life. *Extra Credit* will help you get started on a better financial life.

Randy Heesacker

Randy Heesacker
President
Inceptia

Acknowledgments

In loving memory of my aunt, Tammy (Pratt) Agnew.
Your influence was far greater than you ever imagined.

To Inceptia who provided resources and expertise
for the college financial aid and student loan concepts
and examples I've included in the book.

To Dr. Anna Filippo for helping me in the process of editing.

To the students who have made it this far academically.
I hope this book helps you succeed financially as well.

To all those who have read this book
and helped spread the message to the students and their parents.

To all those who listened to me go on and on about credit,
and to those who helped me in so many ways
by contributing their opinions and feedback.

To my business partners for your support.

To my family for always supporting me
and understanding that I have less available time for them.

To my parents, Rick and LeDeina, for always believing in me.

Finally, to my wife, Christy, for her constant support
and understanding as I spent many hours
on the computer preparing this book for publication.
I could never ask for a more incredible person by my side.

Introduction

In today's economy, knowledge is power. Those who have the ability to understand how to use their money, and more importantly how to keep it, will pull through one of the worst economies since the Great Depression.

My message is simple. Credit is a tool that can be used to create or destroy, just like a hammer. If you try to use credit without really knowing how, then you will be likely to destroy. You can hurt your own credit, hurt your relationships, and hurt your chances for success. Everyone needs to know how to use credit, and when not to use it.

The analogy that I like to use is how winning in sports requires knowing the rules of the game, and having a good coach. If you are playing on a team where nobody else knows how to play, then getting advice from your teammates may actually hurt your game instead of helping it. If you have a coach who understands the rules, understands how to get better, and understands how the other team will try to beat you, then you have a real chance of winning. Of course you have to listen to your coach.

This book is really the first step towards having a coach to really "show you the ropes" so to speak. The best part is that I do not require any drills, or speed workouts. After reading this book you should be that much closer to understanding the basics of credit cards, debit cards, and more. Please don't stop here. Take courses, read other books and articles in print and on the web. Find the right coach/mentor. It will be your quickest way to financial success.

Good luck in your freshman year and beyond!

Bill Pratt

Thing #1

How Your
Money Works

Chapter 1

The importance of understanding how money works

For the first time in your life you will be on your own and be able to make your own decisions without direct parental input. Unfortunately, you will also have to bear the consequences of those decisions. I'm not talking about drugs, alcohol, or STDs. I'm talking about the number one reason students drop out of college. I'm talking about the number one cause of divorce in the United States. I'm talking about the number one reason people get stuck in the middle class. I'm talking about debt.

What you are about to learn will save you thousands of dollars over the next four years, and tens of thousands of dollars over your lifetime. I know. I've been there. I've made the mistakes so you don't have to. I was an economics major and business minor yet I never really learned anything about the real-life practical application of personal finance; how to handle money, credit cards, and debt.

Six years and one Master's degree later, I became a Vice President at a major credit card company and saw how they marketed on college campuses. I also understand how they make their money by keeping you poor.

Fortunately, I researched and read hundreds of books on personal finances. I browsed hundreds of personal finance websites, and read thousands... literally thousands... of personal finance articles. Most of them had the same or similar advice. Many of them were wrong, and I'll tell you why.

I created spreadsheet after spreadsheet, and did the math. Every single spreadsheet looked perfect. I wish I could say that I was able to quickly pay off my debt after college and be completely done with it in three years... but I can't. Despite all of my reading, and all my spreadsheets, something was still not working right... my attitude towards money.

> 38% of students who drop out of school do so because of debt/financial pressure, making it the number one reason, compared to 28% of students dropping out due to academic failure.

It turns out that knowing the math behind the numbers was not enough. There was something more to money than just the math. Personal finances are personal. Then it finally hit me. Money is based on behavior. Until I learned to change my money behavior, I kept outspending my earnings. I'd get a pay raise and I'd spend 110% of it. That cycle continued until my wife and I got fed up with owing money. So we made some spending changes and finally paid off our credit card debt. Then when my wife stopped working for a while the debt came back... because I had not really broken my spending habits - the very habits that started when I was in college.

I was always frugal as a child. My family usually made fun of me for saving and never spending. I always knew I wanted to do something great with my life one day but never had a clear vision of what that really was. The one thing I did know was that everything requires money. College was the first time I ever borrowed money and it didn't end there. It started with college loans, and then crept into a car payment, then eventually into one credit card, then two, then three.

I want to help you avoid doing what I did. I want you to know your limitations and not borrow when you don't have to. I want you to handle your money and your debt responsibly. I want you to be able to live like a college student, but spend like an adult.

There was something more to money than just the math.
Personal finances are personal.
Then it finally hit me. Money is based on behavior.

After reading this book, you will be among the most educated adults, armed with so much information the credit card companies will not know what hit them. For the first time, you will be playing a game with the banking industry where you will finally know all the rules. The odds have always been stacked in the bank's favor because they knew the rules of the game, but never shared them with you.

Are you ready to get started? If you play or have ever tried to play a sport, you quickly find out how important it is to know the rules of the game. The first time I pitched baseball in high school, I didn't understand the balk rule. I didn't know that when a runner was on first base, the right handed pitcher cannot turn his shoulders towards first in order to check on the runner. I learned that one the hard way. The runner got to go to second.

It's tough to even *watch* a game when you don't know the rules, much less play it. I'll bet one of the most common questions people ask during the Super Bowl is, "Why did the referee make *that* call?" You can't win a game if you don't know the rules. In sports, everybody starts with zero and the team with the most points wins. The only way you are able to earn points is to first know the rules of the game. That's how money works as well.

But what if you already have a job lined up or have money from your parents or through student loans or scholarships? Do you remember the first time you played the game of Monopoly™? You sat down and were handed a bunch of cash. Then you rolled the dice and started playing the game. But you probably didn't do too well your first time. Do you know why? Because you didn't know the rules of the game.

Even if you got lucky and kept landing on the right properties, you didn't play as effectively as possible because nobody showed you how. If you were lucky, some of your friends helped explain the rules as the game went along or maybe you read the directions before you started playing.

There are four ways to improve your game: 1) You can have someone explain the rules and strategies of the game; 2) You can learn by experience; 3) You can research it on your own; 4) You can have someone coach you. While having all four strategies are necessary for success, having someone explain the rules and having a coach are the two fastest ways to get better and win.

Regardless of whether you start out with money or nothing at all, you still have to know the rules to win. Otherwise, you will just lose it all, waiting for the next time you get to pass 'Go' to collect your $200. Or, for college students, waiting until your next paycheck or the next deposit into your account from your parents.

Think of this book as your first rule book about money. It is your first play book. Your coach's thoughts on paper. No matter your situation, my guess is that you want to know how money works. You want to know the rules of money, credit, and debt so you can win, or at least so you don't get totally embarrassed running the wrong way with the ball.

Why is it important to know how money works?

_____

_____

_____

_____

What steps can you take to learn about money?

_____

_____

_____

_____

Notes:

_____

_____

_____

_____

_____

_____

_____

Chapter 2

What is a credit score?

Well, I am sure you have seen all of the commercials recently about credit scores. The question is, "What exactly is a credit score, what is it used for, and how does it affect you as a college student?" Credit scores are similar to a report card, except instead of measuring how good you are in your classes, it measures how good you are with your money. So who uses the score and how will it affect you?

Credit scores are used by banks to determine if they will lend you money. Assume for a moment that you do not take care of your credit. This means if you plan to get a new car while you are in college or after you graduate you may have to buy whatever you can afford with cash since the banks will not loan you any money. If you are lucky enough to have a car already then no problem, right?

Actually, insurance companies also look at credit scores to determine if they want to insure you. Yes, auto insurance companies use credit scores as one factor to determine if they are willing to insure you at all, or if they will charge you higher rates.

Looks like you will have to bum a ride to your job interviews since you cannot afford to drive your own car. At least once you get a decent job you can pay off debt and repair your credit and save for a car... Or did I forget to mention that employers also look at your credit score? They want to see if you are truly responsible with your money. People who are irresponsible with their own money and with their own lives are unlikely to be very responsible at work with other people's money. This means you are without a ride and without a job. It will be tough to hang onto your own place.

Except, of course, landlords *also* check your credit score. If you have a bad credit score then landlords do not want to risk that you may skip out on rent payments. Ouch! I guess this means you will be stuck moving in with your parents after graduation. And you can forget about buying a place of your own. With no job, no money, no car and no credit, you are starting out in really bad shape.

See, the entire financial industry understands that people with messy finances also lead messy lives. In other words, the way you handle money is a reflection of your character at a deeper level.

So what exactly makes up a credit score? Your credit score consists of five main pieces of information. Your payment history, the amounts you owe, the length of history, new credit, and types of credit.

1. Payment History

Your payment history represents 35% of your score. It includes past due items, how long they have been past due, and any delinquencies or judgments that are a result of being very, very late on your payments or simply never paying them at all. This is why it is important that if you borrow money, make sure you have the ability to pay it back on time.

2. Amounts Owed

The amounts you owe represent 30% of your score. This means multiple loans and credit cards with large amounts owed can hurt your score even if you are making all the payments on time. Banks understand that the more debt you have, the harder it will be for you to make your payments if something goes wrong (loss of a job, major unexpected emergency, etc.). They also look at the proportion of your credit that is being used. This means if you have two credit cards, each with a $1,000 credit limit and one card is maxed out and the other is not being used, you are using 50% of your available credit. Some people mistakenly close their unused card to help their score, but if you close the unused card you would now be using 100% of your available credit and your score will go down.

3. Length of Credit History

The length of your credit history represents 15% of your score. Keep in mind you must have credit that is reported for at least six months in order to even have a credit score. The length of credit history looks at the time since you opened your accounts and the time since you last had activity on them.

Ask yourself would you rather have a surgeon who has 10 years of experience or one who just graduated from medical school? The same concept applies to credit. From the bank's perspective, if they are going to loan you money the longer history you have of proving that you will repay your debt, the less risky you seem. On the other hand if you have never missed a payment and only have one year of credit history, it only proves you can make payments for a short period of time. You may not have had a chance to go through life's ups and downs while still maintaining your payments.

4. New Credit

New credit represents 10% of your score. It considers the number of new accounts and how many times you have asked for credit recently. If you have five accounts, but they are all new, this could mean you are either just starting out or you suddenly found yourself in need to borrow a lot. Each time you apply for credit (loan, credit card, etc.) it gets tracked. If you do it too frequently then it appears you are desperate for credit which also makes you look bad.

5. Types of Credit

The remaining 10% of your score is made up of the types of credit you have. A mix of different types of credit is good. If you only have four credit cards and nothing else, you only have one type of credit; which is revolving credit. On the other hand, if you have a loan and a credit card then you have at least two types of credit; a revolving loan and an installment loan. This will improve your score as you can demonstrate that you are able to handle different types of debt.

So what can you do to create or improve your score? It is helpful to first look at your credit report. Of course, those TV commercials for free credit reports or scores require you to subscribe to a monthly service that you have to pay for before they will provide your report or score for free.

The only way to really see your credit report for free each year is to go to *www.annualcreditreport.com* and request it from each of the three major credit bureaus; Transunion, Experian, and Equifax. However, you cannot get your score for free, just your report. You can order a credit score for less than $20 from the three credit bureaus or go to *www.MyFico.com* and order your actual FICO score, which is the most commonly used.

If you do find an error, you can dispute the error with the credit bureau and with the creditor that reported the incorrect information. They must investigate it. Send in a letter that identifies the issues. Make sure you send your letters by certified mail so you can prove that they received it and when they received it.

> **The only real free credit reports come from**
> *wwww.annualcreditreport.com.*
> **To see your actual credit score,**
> **you will have to pay a fee.**

I do recommend that you get a credit card while you are in college--if you qualify--with a low maximum credit limit such as $500. Your first credit card can help you establish a credit history. You are likely to want to establish credit while you are still in college so that you will be better able to qualify for a large loan when you need it such as a car or a house later on. Getting a credit card is really one of the first steps for college students to begin building their credit history.

I do not recommend getting your card during your freshman year. You have too much adjusting to do, so don't risk overdoing it. You may consider applying for a credit card your sophomore year if you have used a debit card for at least one full year, otherwise wait until your junior year. The key is to understand how to use it *correctly* before you get one. This way you will have almost two full years of credit history by the time you graduate. You can also get a small personal loan from a bank or credit union to establish a credit history. This will give you two different types of credit and could help boost your score.

Why is it important to know how credit works?

_____

_____

_____

_____

List the five components that make up your credit score:

_____

_____

_____

_____

_____

Notes:

_____

_____

_____

_____

_____

_____

_____

Thing #2

How to Use Credit Cards

Chapter 3

What is a credit card?

A credit card is a way for banks to move money around electronically. You swipe the black stripe on the back of your card which has all kinds of information (account number, expiration date, etc.), it goes through an electronic network, talks to the bank that issued the card, finds out if you have that much available credit and then tells the Point-of-Sale machine that it's okay to let you make your purchase.

Of course they even give you the option to spend more than your available credit, and then they can charge you an over-the-limit fee. That's just one of the many fees they like to charge in order to cushion their bottom line. They also like to charge late fees. These two fees can end up costing you more in a year than what you pay in interest! Being just a little bit late or paying even $1 less than the minimum payment can lead to a late fee of $25 or more.

What does it mean to use a credit card? It's a way to get an immediate loan for cash you don't have. That sounds exciting at first. You get to spend money that you don't have. If you earned $100 last week, but you have a credit card with a $1,000 limit, then you could spend $1,100! Sounds like a great deal. What's the problem? The problem is you will have to pay it back… with interest. So what, right? What's a few bucks interest for the "privilege" of spending the money before you had to earn it? I mean it won't hurt to do it just once, right? Maybe twice.

Maybe I'll just use it my freshman year; then I'll get a good job next summer to pay it off. The problem is that spending is addictive. Spending money actually releases certain chemicals in your brain (e.g. endorphins), causing a temporary "high." What happens after you are done spending? It leads to a small "crash." The more money you are going to spend on a purchase (such as a car) the more chemicals released, thus the more intense the "high." The after-effect you will experience is a greater "low" or crash. When people spend a lot of money on something like a vacation, or a car, or a house, they experience what is called "buyer's remorse." Once the "high" goes away, you are left with a big debt and time to second-guess your purchase.

> When people spend a lot of money on something,
> they experience what is called "buyer's remorse."
> Once the high goes away, you are left with a
> big debt and time to second-guess your purchase.

Once you charge that first $1,000 on your credit card, you have now established a lifestyle where you are accustomed to spending more than you make. You have shifted your lifestyle up a notch… temporarily. The only way to keep that up is to spend another thousand dollars. But that will just get you to where you were before. Besides, you are also going to have to start making payments from earlier spending, which eats up your income. So really you need to borrow a little more than $1,000 in order to maintain your growing lifestyle. Hmm… sounds like the $1,000 credit card works like a gateway drug.

Just as certain drugs, such as marijuana, are classified as gateway drugs, so is your first credit card. Let me explain. For many people who want to "innocently" smoke marijuana, they enjoy the high that they get. The problem is they begin to crave the marijuana and many go back and use it again and again. But their body gets used to the chemicals and they no longer experience the same high as before. So they start to seek a stronger drug. Then they get used to that drug... The next thing you know, the "casual" marijuana user is addicted to crack.

While the health consequences are certainly different, there is a correlation between the addictions. You can literally get addicted to spending.

People with $1,000 make $100 mistakes; people with $10,000 make $1,000 mistakes; and people with $100,000 make $10,000 mistakes. You have started a lifelong habit of saying, "I want to spend it now, and earn it later." But when later comes, do you really think you are interested in *not* spending your next paycheck, but using it to pay off something you *already* bought instead?

> Your first credit card is like a "gateway drug."
> Once you get used to spending more than you make,
> you want to spend more and more and open
> additional credit cards just to get by.

Let's say that your payment is $40 per month. That means that if you only borrow $1,000 your freshman year and make just a $40 monthly payment, you will not pay it off until your senior year. You will have had to sacrifice some of your spending money each month along the way just to pay it off.

Don't get caught up thinking you'll just pay it off once you get a "real job" after college. In my book, *The Graduate's Guide to Life and Money*, I explain that the average college graduate overestimates his or her starting salary by 44%. In addition, you will only get to keep about 65%-75% of your paycheck after taxes, insurance, retirement, etc. That assumes you are even able to find a job. Most students take about six months after graduation to find a good job.

Have you noticed that we are constantly bombarded with commercials from credit card companies? They support sporting events and all the hit television shows in primetime. They make a fortune off of us, so they can afford these large commercial campaigns. Even Barbie™ came with a credit card for a while.

> The average college graduate overestimates his or her starting salary by 44%. In addition, you will only get to keep about 65%-75% of your paycheck after taxes, insurance, retirement, etc.

Credit cards are convenient. It is almost a requirement to purchase gas with a credit card these days. You can make online purchases with your credit card. You don't even have to have any cash on you to make purchases anymore. If you lose your wallet, you are only out some convenience (and your driver's license). You will not be out any money if you report your lost card. But be very careful. You will lose a whole lot more money in interest payments and overpayments on credit cards during your lifetime than you will from losing your wallet with cash in it.

What you will start to notice is that every store has their own credit card and they are always pushing you to use it. "Will you be paying for that on your Store charge card today?" Why is that? Stores want you to apply for and use their branded card so they pay little to no transaction fees. They also want you to apply for and use their cobranded card (with the Visa or MasterCard logo) because they get paid when you get that card. Plus, statistics show that the average shopper spends 18% more per transaction when using a credit card than when using cash. Department stores have created a vicious cycle.

First, they offer sales and discounts, but only if you make the purchase with their card. In addition, if you sign up that day, you'll save 10% off your entire purchase. Now they got you.

They have your mailing address. Now they can mail you additional offers just for using their credit card in the store. Now you want to use their card again to get your discount. Now they have you spending more money, at their store particularly, usually on items you would not have gone to purchase except you did receive that coupon in the mail… Not to mention you now have yet another card that you have make sure you pay off every month as department store cards usually charge a very high interest rate (20%+) for balances not paid in full!

> **Statistics show that the average shopper spends 18% more per transaction when using a credit card than when using cash.**

The department stores normally get paid for every card they open, and the credit card companies make profits off of people not paying their balances. This is very lucrative for the credit card companies, so believe it when I tell you: despite your best intentions, at some point you will not be able to pay off the entire balance in one month, and then you pay interest. Once you start to not pay it all off, it gets easier and easier to not pay off your card in a given month.

The biggest "convenience" offered by credit cards is that you can buy something now without going home to get the money or waiting until you get your next paycheck. But that is exactly how they get people to purchase more. When you leave the store without buying an item, there is a very high chance that by the time you get home and get your money you will change your mind or find something more important to spend your money on. That is why the store wants you to use your credit card to make your purchase right away, before you have a chance to change your mind. You need to know how the game is played in order to have a chance of winning.

What is a credit card?

_____

_____

_____

_____

What makes a credit card dangerous?

_____

_____

_____

_____

Notes:

_____

_____

_____

_____

_____

_____

_____

Chapter 4

The top 10 tricks used by credit card companies

B efore we start talking about the tricks that credit card companies use, let's discuss how they make their money. Then everything else will make a lot more sense.

There are three main sources of income for credit card companies. The first is through the transactions. Every time you swipe your credit card, a small percentage of your total bill (usually around 2%) goes to the credit card company, not the store owner. For instance, if you pay $100 for an iPod and use your credit card, the store will only get $98 while the credit card company will get $2. That doesn't sound like much money but if you think about all the transactions taking place in the world at any given moment it adds up.

Since credit card companies are basically banks, you have to assume they do not make enough profit from transaction fees to be happy... and you would be right. When you make a purchase, you are borrowing money. Now, if you pay it off during the grace period (usually about 21 - 25 days), there is no interest. However, if you are unable to pay off the entire balance during the grace period, you will be charged interest. Most adults are already accustomed to paying interest on other things anyway. If you borrow money to buy a car or a house, you will pay interest. If you borrow money on a credit card, you will pay interest. Is this the same thing? Well, it's similar but the interest rates are *way* different. Instead of paying the 5% - 8% interest rates you see for homes and cars, you will pay as much as 16% - 24%! We'll discuss interest more in the next chapter.

The third way credit card companies make their money is through fees. You can pay late fees, over-the-limit fees, cash advance fees, balance transfer fees, and even an annual fee on some cards. So what's wrong with fees? Mostly, they cost you money. Would you randomly take $25 and put it in a shredder? I don't know about you, but when I was in college $25 was a lot of money. I would have rather gone to the movies and bought a pizza with that money instead. That is what you could pay for being one day late on your credit card payment.

Are the fees legitimate? Well, they are all spelled out for you on the original contract and even more detail is provided when they send the actual card to you in the mail. So in that sense, the credit card companies are doing nothing illegal. They just know how to play the game. Until now, nobody told you the rules.

Now for the top 10 tricks used by credit card companies:

1. Use your card for everything

Now that you know how credit card companies make their money, let's see how they "trick" you. There is no real trickery when it comes to simply swiping your card, unless you consider all the ads encouraging you to use your credit card for absolutely everything. Their goal is to get you to make every purchase with their card, not pay it off every month, and keep your balance close to but not over the limit. They want you to be able to make the payments… but just barely.

2. You get points for spending money

Aside from all the advertisements teasing you into wanting to use your card for just about everything, they also try to entice you with their reward points. For every dollar you spend you get a reward point. For every 1,000 points you can get a $10 gift card. So you had to spend $1,000 just to get a $10 gift card? If you pay just one month of interest at 18% with a balance of $1,000 you will pay them $15 in interest charges. Just one month! You had to spend a total of $1,000 and you get $10, but one time you can't pay off your whole balance and you have given them $15! No wonder we can't ever seem to get ahead.

3. The 0% balance transfer

What a great deal! You can transfer the balances from your other cards and pay 0% in interest. It's seems like such a good deal, after all you are borrowing money for free. Of course, if credit card companies let you borrow money for free, how would they make any money? They are betting that you will mess up or not pay it off very timely. Don't worry for their sake, because they are usually right! And in the event you do not mess up, it was still not free. Why is this considered a trick? The next three tricks tell the story:

4. Balance transfer fee of 4%

When you look at the details (also called fine print) you will see that there is a balance transfer fee, usually of 4% with a minimum of $10 and no maximum. What does this mean? This means that if you transfer $1,000 to the zero percent interest card, you will pay a transfer fee of $40. So you are pre-paying interest in a sense. The interest rate is substituted by the transfer fee.

Since most zero percent transfer offers last less than a year, it is like paying more than 4% in interest. A good deal? Yes. Free? No. Also, since the minimum was $10, if you only transfer $100 you would still pay $10, which is 10%. So never transfer such a small amount. Just pay it off. Sell something on eBay® if you have to.

5. 0% or low rates that you lose with one mistake

Another card favorite is the little clause that states that if you make any mistake such as charging over your credit limit or you pay late even once, then you lose the 0% or low introductory rate and your card defaults to the regular rate, usually around 16% or higher. If you make another mistake, your rate can easily jump to 24% or higher. Fortunately you will have to be 60 days late before they can raise your interest rate.

If you do find that you are about to run late, but are still within the timeframe, you can usually call and make an emergency payment, which will cost you about $35. Unfortunately, this may be your best option if you are about to lose a low interest rate on a large balance.

6. Introductory teaser rates on purchases

If you have not seen the ads and the mailings, then you soon will. Credit card offers are notorious for offering very low introductory rates to hook you in, but they only last a short period of time. Who cares if you pay just 3% for six months, if you keep a balance on there for a year? In light of four years of school, what are three or six months of low rates? Especially when you consider that for most people, they continue to charge and increase their balance as time goes on.

So you get the low introductory rate when you first get the card and have a very small balance, but as your balance increases the rate goes up (after the introductory period). It won't take long before that low rate is long forgotten. Of course a new card will come along and offer to transfer your balance to their card at 0% for six months (see Trick #4).

7. Lowest interest rate balance gets paid first

Sometimes credit card balances are split among various different interest rates. For instance, you could have a 0% transfer balance, a 18% purchase balance, and a 24% cash advance balance (but not if you took my advice).When you make your minimum credit card payment it will go towards the part of your balance with the lowest interest rate (in this case the 0%).

What happens if you have $1,000 at 0% and then you charge another $1,000 at the regular interest rate? When you send in your minimum payment, the money is applied to the portion at 0% but not the $1,000 at regular rates.

"So what?" you ask. The interest that you owed on the $1,000 (let's assume 18% interest rate so you would owe $15.00 in interest) accumulates. Next month you owe interest on $1,015.00. The next month you owe interest on $1,030.23. Where did the other 23 cents come from? You paid interest on your interest! While 23 cents does not sound like much now, each month the compound interest that you pay grows exponentially. At the end of one year, your $1,000 purchase balance will have grown to $1,195.62.

The great news is that any *extra* you pay on your card must be applied to the balance with the largest interest rate. So to avoid getting hurt by this "trick," simply pay more than the minimum.

8. No grace period on purchases

Most people justify using their credit card because they "have a 30 day grace period" before they are required to pay it off. First of all, most grace periods have been reduced to around 21 days. However, if you are already carrying a balance on your card, you do not get a grace period.

In other words, if you already have an existing balance carried over from a prior month (you are already paying interest) then you start paying interest on your new purchases from the moment you make that purchase. Even if you pay off the card at the end of the current month, you will have paid interest on your purchase if you waited until your next statement due date.

The irony is that if you made the purchase for the reward points (which usually equate to about 1%) and your credit card interest rate is higher than 12%, you paid more than 1% in interest to get 1% in points. Not a good deal at all.

9. Increasing credit limit

How can you get in too much trouble when your credit limit is only $1,000? I mean $1,000 is a lot of money, but it is within reason right? If I keep making my payments on time everything should be okay, right?

Wrong. Because of your stellar record, the credit card company feels that you are entitled to a higher credit limit. So they will probably increase your limit to $1,500. They may continue to raise your credit limit without asking you by $500 or $1,000 at a time every six months or so, especially if you continue to stay near your newest limit. By the time you graduate, you may have a $5,000 credit limit on one card, or have a $2,000 - $3,000 limit on a couple of different cards.

By luring you in with such a small, low-risk credit limit they get you addicted to spending money you don't have. Once you reach your max, you can't spend more than you make, unless they extend more credit to you. The best way to avoid this issue is to call them and graciously decline the increased credit limit. Ask them to keep your credit limit at $1,000.

10. Decreasing minimum payments

One of the key differences between a loan payment and a credit card payment is that a loan payment is fixed (the same amount every month) while a credit card payment changes according to your current balance. For instance, if you charge $1,000 on your 18% credit card, your minimum payment will be around $35. If you pay $35 per month your credit card will be paid off in about three years. However, credit card minimum payments decrease as your balance decreases.

Once your balance gets below $970, your payment drops to $34, which will stretch out your "loan" a little longer. Your minimum payment continues to get lower as your balance gets smaller, resulting in stretching out your "loan" even more. By the time your balance reaches $500, your minimum payment will only be around $18. The end result is a credit card that takes five years to pay off (instead of three years) and with more than $500 in interest!

What are some of the tricks used by credit card companies?

_____

_____

_____

_____

_____

_____

_____

How can you avoid being tricked?

_____

_____

_____

_____

Notes:

_____

_____

_____

_____

Thing #3

How to Handle Debt

Chapter 5

What is debt?

Debt is when you owe something to someone else. For the purpose of this book, we are going to discuss financial debt, but you could also owe somebody time (I promise I'll watch that movie with you next weekend) or a service (I'll cook Thanksgiving dinner this year).

If you borrowed money for your college education through student loans, then you owe money. With most federal student loans you don't have to begin making payments until six months after you graduate, but that does not mean you don't owe the money. You borrowed money to pay for college so you will have to pay it back with interest when you graduate.

If your parents are paying for your education, then you owe them in a completely different way (see earlier examples). I'm not saying all parents use guilt to manipulate you, but don't be surprised if you are expected to spend more time with them during the holidays or summer vacation, or anytime you are off from school. Despite getting used to being on your own, your parents may feel they are "owed" your time and consideration since they are paying for your education. (Just a heads up for your first summer vacation.) Now back to money.

As you can see using the student loan example, it doesn't matter *when* you have to pay for something; if you owe somebody money you are in debt. You already received the services but have not paid for it yet.

Sometimes you may owe zero percent on something. For instance, some car dealerships offer 0% financing on new vehicles. Is this debt? Of course it is. You have the car but have not yet paid for *all* of it. Even if you are not required to pay any interest you must pay back what you borrowed. Now you are in a situation where you can't stop earning money (e.g. you can't quit your job), because you owe your money to somebody else.

> **Whether you have to pay it right away or wait until later and if you are being charged interest or not, owing money to somebody else for products or services provided that you did not yet pay for is debt.**

Other examples are the so-called 6-month or 12-month same-as-cash offers, which are usually available through home improvement stores and furniture stores. Even though you are allowed to pay off the whole balance within a certain time-frame and not pay any interest, you still owe the money. You still get to take the item home without paying for it. You are expected to pay for it within the next six or 12 months.

Whether you have to pay it right away or wait until later and if you are being charged interest or not, owing money to somebody else for products or services provided that you did not yet pay for is debt. You would think that is pretty clear and simple enough, but apparently for many people it is not.

A friend of mine owed over $10,000 on his car and credit cards combined. He came to me one day and said, "I got rid of all my debt." At first I was amazed. That was a lot of money to pay off in such a short amount of time, so I asked him how he did it. He replied, "I consolidated everything I owed into one personal loan." Sadly, I pointed out that before the loan he owed $10,000 and now that he consolidated, he still owed $10,000. The difference was that his interest rate was better and he only owed it to one bank, but he still owed it.

The lesson here is that consolidating your debt is not paying it off. Transferring balances from one credit card to another is not paying it off. Paying the money you owe somebody, with the promised amount of interest, is the only way to actually pay off your debt.

What is debt?

_____

_____

_____

_____

Why is debt consolidation not the same as paying it off?

_____

_____

_____

_____

Notes:

_____

_____

_____

_____

_____

_____

_____

Chapter 6

Why is debt bad?

O h, let me count the ways. Debt is bad for so many reasons. Any time you add debt you are adding risk. While risk is not always bad you want to make sure you only take necessary risks and that you understand all of the potential consequences.

1. Debt takes away your choices

Think about it. What if you are offered the perfect job in the perfect location, but the pay is not very high. Still, it may be your dream job of testing video games or choosing the fall line of clothes for a retailer. But if you have high student loans and a lot of credit card debt, the low salary will mean you cannot afford to take the perfect job.

2. Debt reflects on your character

Now stop here for a moment. Do you remember earlier when I said that it finally hit me that money was a behavioral issue, not just a math issue? The way you handle money is a reflection of your character at a deeper level. Think about it. The banks, insurance agents, landlords and employers have all figured out that people who are not responsible with their money are also not responsible in other areas of their lives. Take that lesson to heart. If you are in financial trouble, there may be deeper issues at stake.

> The way you handle money is a reflection of your character at a deeper level.

3. Debt can affect your ability to get hired!

Remember our discussion about credit scores? Employers are not only checking social media sites but also checking credit reports as a way of measuring how responsible people are. Statistically people with bad credit tend to make for bad or problem employees. How ironic would it be if spending more money than you can handle kept you from getting the very job that would give you the ability to pay it off?

> Employers are checking credit reports as a way of measuring how responsible people are. What that means to you is that irresponsible spending could prevent you from getting a job!

4. Debt prevents wealth

Do you know what your greatest wealth creating tool is at your disposal? It's your income. No matter what the stock market is doing, or what direction the economy is going, having a solid income can help you continue to build wealth. Do you know the number one way to neutralize your income? Debt.

If you have $2,000 coming in every month, but your debt payments are $1,500, then you really only have $500 disposable income coming in. It's hard to build wealth when you have just $500 per month to work with (which you will need to pay for all of your regular expenses such as food, utilities, etc.). Even if you only have $500 worth of debt payments that means you have $500 less to invest towards your future.

5. Debt creates more debt

What happens if you keep borrowing? You think you can't because you are maxed out? Well, you'll start getting additional credit card offers and your other card will increase your credit limit, usually $500 - $1,000 at a time. You could keep borrowing and borrowing, easily working your way up to $5,000 in credit card debt by the time you graduate. Some people are able to get in over their head owing more than $10,000. This is in addition to college loans, car loans, etc.

Next thing you know your monthly payments are so high the only way to pay your bills is to use your credit cards until they are maxed out. You will be looking for credit card offers, personal loans like the ones advertised on television, or other poor alternatives such as car title loans. This is a downhill financial cycle in which I hope you never find yourself trapped.

6. Debt creates stress

During an economic downturn, who is affected the most? People with debt or people who are out of debt? While any economic recession or downturn is scary to most individuals and families, those who owe lots of money are the ones most affected and stressed.

If you owe nothing on your car, and owe nothing on your home, and owe nothing on credit cards, what do you have to fear if the price of your house goes down? What happens if you lose your job? Sure, you need to find another job to make enough money to eat and pay the utilities. But it is easy to find a new job right away that pays enough to cover the essentials. It is very difficult and stressful to find a job right away that pays enough to cover the essentials, plus the rent, car, student loan, and credit card payments.

7. Debt takes away your choices!!

I realize I already mentioned this one, but it warrants repeating. Debt takes away your choices. You can't quit your job if your boss is a tyrant, you can't take a summer off to backpack in Europe, and you can't go on a mission trip to Brazil. You have to keep working to pay for your debt *before* you can start saving the money to pay for your other options. Would you like to start your own business? Would you like to make a positive impact through generous giving? How can you help support your favorite cause if you cannot yet support yourself and your spending habits?

In our society, we are all about choices. You can choose four different types of cheeses for your sandwich, 50 flavors of ice cream, or 20 flavors of coffee. Cars, cell phones, iPods, laptop computers and even washers & dryers come in multiple colors. We love choices. That's one of the ways we celebrate our freedom. Unfortunately, too many of us voluntarily give up our freedom by giving away our choices. We *choose* to spend more than we have today and have to make up for it tomorrow, and the next day, and the day after. Choose debt or choose freedom; it's up to you.

Why is debt bad?

_____

_____

_____

_____

_____

_____

Explain how the way you manage your money can reflect how you act in other areas of your life.

_____

_____

_____

_____

_____

_____

Notes:

_____

_____

_____

Chapter 7

What do I do once I get into debt?

So far, we have discussed why to avoid debt, how to resist credit card offers, and so forth, but what happens if it is too late? What if you already have debt? Don't let it worry you too much, because if you are serious about getting out of debt and cleaning up your credit it is quite possible to do it in a very short period of time. The key is that you really have to *want* to do it.

You will have to choose how intensely you want to get out of debt. You can casually adjust your spending levels and slowly get out of debt by naturally paying off what you owe. If you want to step it up a bit, there are more aggressive ways to cut your expenses and increase your income in order to pay off your debt even quicker, while still maintaining a somewhat familiar lifestyle. Of course, you can also go full throttle and radically change your lifestyle, work at least two jobs in the summer and wipe out almost any amount of student credit card debt in about one year. The choice is yours.

No matter what approach to debt elimination you want to choose, the first step is always to stop getting into more debt. When you reach this point it makes the most sense to stop carrying your credit card with you everywhere. Don't use the excuse that you need it for emergencies. After all, how has that worked out for you so far? That's why you are reading this section now.

There are a ton of strategies to reduce your expenses, but the first and easiest is to eliminate or significantly reduce (again, depends on how intense you want to go) your dining out. Americans spend over $500 billion each year dining out. That's why we are broke *and* overweight. If you have a job and usually eat lunch or dinner out, start packing. Don't forget to use leftovers if you have access to a microwave.

> **Americans spend over $580 billion dining out.**
> **That's why we are broke *and* overweight**

Depending on your level of involvement in school activities, you can get a part-time job in the evenings, and on weekends. You may qualify for an on-campus job. Some are based on need, and others are just based on school funding availability. Ask around. It will be easier to work on campus in the computer lab, for instance, than to have to drive to the mall.

If you purchased your own car (not one from your parents) and you are making payments, ask yourself how much of your income is being eaten up by car payments. For the real intense debt eliminators, it may be time to admit you made a mistake when you bought your car, and sell it. Replace it with an older or less sporty model, or buy a beater (good engine, ugly body). At least with a beater you can give it a name, and your friends will make fun of it *with* you instead of behind your back.

Be careful if you get a second job. Too many people will get a second job, and then increase their spending because they have a second income. All that does is trap you into needing both jobs. The money from the second job should *only* be used for paying off debt.

At this stage you should not even consider bankruptcy. First of all, you made a promise when you borrowed the money to repay it. Don't make your first commitment as an adult a failed commitment.

A number of people who have filed for bankruptcy did not need to do so; they were just advised to do so by a bankruptcy attorney, because that is what they get paid to do. Most importantly, federal student loans cannot be discharged if filing for bankruptcy. That means if you are $25,000 in debt, and $20,000 is from student loans, you can only get rid of the other $5,000. Now doesn't it seem silly to file for bankruptcy for $5,000 of debt? If it does not seem silly now, it will in a few years when you look back on it.

Because bankruptcy stays on your record for seven years (or 10 years in some cases), you will have trouble getting a car or a house in the future. Besides, if you think owing a lot of money relative to your income is bad for your credit, try declaring bankruptcy. That will leave a serious mark for years to come. Besides, declaring bankruptcy is very draining emotionally. Instead, keep your chin up, eyes forward, and get back in the game!

Here is the easiest way to get out of debt:

1. Stop spending more than you earn.
2. Put all of your extra money onto the debt with the lowest balance, not the debt with the highest interest rate.
3. Once that debt is paid off, use all the money you had been paying on that debt (the minimum payment plus the extra that you were paying) and add it to the next highest debt.
4. Repeat that process until all debt is eliminated.

As I said before, it is up to you to decide how aggressively you want to pay down your debt. Using this approach could take 10 years or it could take 10 months. It's up to you to decide if you want to sacrifice a lot for a short period of time or sacrifice a little over a much longer period of time.

How quickly could I get out of debt?

_____

_____

_____

_____

What steps are required in order to pay off my debt?

_____

_____

_____

_____

Notes:

_____

_____

_____

_____

_____

_____

_____

_____

Thing #4

How to Use
Your Debit Card

Chapter 8

What is a debit card?

Great question. What is a debit card? A debit card uses the same networks as credit cards. That is why you will find the VISA or MasterCard symbol on most debit cards. When you swipe your debit card, the black strip on the back has information, just like a credit card. The Point-of-Sale machine at the store reads the card, sends information through the network, finds out how much is in your account, and sends that information back to the Point-of-Sale machine as approved or declined.

The key here is that instead of checking how much available credit you have like a credit card does, it checks to see how much money you actually have in your account at that moment. Normally a debit card is linked to a checking account, but it can be linked to a savings account or money market account as well. It can also be linked to other accounts such as a flexible spending account for health insurance, or a meal plan at school.

The main difference between a debit card and a credit card is that you are borrowing money you don't have every time you use a credit card, but with a debit card you are actually using money that you have in your bank account, so you are not borrowing. You are spending your own money. You have to first earn money in order to use a debit card.

A debit card will come with a PIN (Personal Identification Number). A PIN is a four-digit code or password that will allow you to use your card in order to get money out of an ATM, or to get cash back at the store. NEVER share your PIN with anyone and don't write it where someone could find it. That would be like giving someone a blank signed check (we'll discuss checks later) or free access to your bank account.

When you make a purchase at the store you normally have the option of selecting "Credit" or "Debit" or the cashier will ask you to choose one. This is very important. Some banks charge you each time you use your debit card as a debit (where you actually key in your PIN). This sounds crazy, but you can actually use your debit card as a credit card... but not really. This is where it gets more confusing.

> **Some banks charge you each time you use your debit card as a debit & key your PIN.**

Remember earlier when I explained the networks? Well, when you select "Debit" on the swipe machine, the merchant loses a smaller percentage, which means the network and bank do not get as much money per transaction. To make up for that loss, they will charge you 50 cents. That's right, they charge you 50 cents to use your own money! So when given the option, if your bank charges, you want to select "Credit." This does not mean that you are borrowing money with your debit card the way credit cards work. It means that the network and bank are satisfied and you don't have to supplement their greed. Either way money comes directly from your account. The difference is that you did not pay the extra fee.

If you happen to be in a situation where you want to get some cash back with your transaction, then you may want to go ahead and select "Debit", pay the 50 cents (if your bank charges you) and get whatever amount of cash you want back. That means if you go to the store and get a pack of gum, you can get, for example, $40 back in cash as well. Usually you can get anywhere from $10 - $100 back in cash, but it varies depending on the store. Of course when you see your bank statement it will show the store charge for $41 (assuming you chose $40 cash back and the gum was $1 including tax). Then you will see a separate charge for 50 cents, usually labeled as POS fee (meaning Point-of-Sale, which is what they call the credit/debit card machines where you swipe your card).

71% of Americans age 18-24 use a debit card in any given month.

There are three disadvantages of using your debit card to get cash back at the store. The first is that you are paying a fee to use your own money, if your bank is one that charges you for the privilege. The second is that you will not get a statement that shows the balance in your account like you do when you use an ATM. The third is that you will have a much harder time keeping your finances in order because you will start to forget about the $20 here and the $40 there that you were getting back in cash, and then spending on whatever. So please be careful.

Hopefully you can now tell the difference between using your debit card and credit card. One takes money from your existing account, while the other forces you to borrow against money you have not yet earned, and now owe. There are still a few other things that you need to know about debit cards before we move on.

When you use your debit card, you will still spend more money per transaction than you would if you had cash. While debit cards are more similar to cash because the money comes directly from your bank account, you still don't get the full disincentive of spending like you do when you physically open your wallet, and pull out the cash and watch your cash balance disappear in front of your eyes. There is a huge psychological factor in pulling actual cash from your wallet and seeing what is left. Your mind creates a negative response, and in many cases, you are less likely to make a purchase, just because you prefer the comfort of knowing you have cash in your wallet in case something more important comes up. This goes back to what I said about debt, where debt takes away your choices. We naturally like having choices, and having cash on us gives us choices.

Also, if you use your debit card for gasoline, a lot of times you will either see a $1 charge at first (if you look online immediately after you use the card at the pump) or you may see a "block" on your account for around $50-$75 (the amount is based on the average cost to fill up a vehicle). When you swipe your card, the gas station does not know how much gas you will need, so they may "block" $75 of your account just to make sure there is enough to pay for the gas.

> ## 74% of monthly college spending is with cash and debit cards. Only 7 percent is with credit cards.

Within the next two days the portion of the $75 that you did not use will be released, and will be available to you again. This is important because if you have $100 in your account, and you only get $50 in gas, you expect $50 is still available. But if you try to buy something for $50, your card may be declined, since you only have access to $25 thanks to the $75 block. Due to technology efficiencies, the large block on your card is becoming less common, but it may still happen.

Finally, your debit card can be used at almost any ATM where you can simply get cash out of your account. The ATM (Automated Teller Machine) basically lets you withdraw money from your bank account. The banks use a different network than the credit cards, but it works about the same. Information is sent using your password or PIN, the network checks to see how much money is in your account, and then lets you withdraw up to a certain amount (depending on bank policy) assuming it is less than your total account balance.

The main advantage of the ATM is that you will get a receipt that has your current balance. Please be careful with this receipt. First of all, it has the last four (or first four) digits of your account, so don't just leave it lying around. I'm not sure what anyone can do with just those four digits, but let's not take any chances and hand identity thieves a piece of the key to the castle. Also, don't rely entirely on your ATM receipt.

> **If you use an ATM owned by a bank other than your own, you could pay as much as $5 - $6 just to get your own money!**

Sometimes the ATM receipt may reflect your balance as old as two days ago. That means if you made a $50 purchase at the grocery store last night, and then go to the ATM this morning, the balance on your receipt may not reflect the $50 you spent last night, so your account balance appears to be $50 higher than it really is. If you keep a relatively low balance in your account, as most college students do, this can be dangerous. It is important to monitor your balance online.

I have another acronym for ATM; Always Takes Money. What do I mean? Remember how you may pay 50 cents to use your debit card as a debit card at the store? Well, you will pay much more than that to use your debit card at the ATM, if the

ATM is owned by another bank. You'll have to check with your bank to see what its policy is, because every bank and credit union is different.

The standard is usually that you do not pay a fee if you use the ATM provided by your bank or credit union. However, if you use another bank's ATM, you will pay anywhere from $2 - $4, and that is just what *they* charge. *Your* bank may also charge another $2-$4 because you used another bank's ATM. That means you could end up paying as much as $8 just to get to your own money! No wonder there are so many ATMs around.

The banks can charge because they own the machines. For the convenience of having access to fast cash, you are paying a fee. Since the banks have to communicate to each other, they can each charge you a fee. If you pay $5 and withdraw $20 from the ATM that is like being charged a 300% fee (annualized). Look at it another way, if you withdraw $20 every month and pay a $5 fee each time, you are "donating" 20% of your money to the bank. If you pay $5 and withdraw $100 you are still paying a 5% fee (or 60% annualized). What if you only need $40 per week and use another bank's ATM each time you withdraw money? During the course of the year, you will have spent $260 in transaction fees at ATMs. I don't know about you, but most college kids could do a lot with that $260, so don't waste it at the ATM.

If you do find yourself using the ATM a lot, then make sure you use the one belonging to your bank, which is why it is a good idea to choose a bank or credit union near your school or work. If not, then try to make fewer withdrawals, each at larger amounts. At least then you will minimize the damage. Using our last example, if you pull out $160 once each month instead of $40 per week, you'll spend approximately $60 instead of the $260. You will still be throwing away $60, but that's $200 less.

What is a debit card?

_____

_____

_____

_____

What are some ways you can avoid paying fees when using your debit card?

_____

_____

_____

_____

Notes:

_____

_____

_____

_____

Chapter 9

Why is cash better?

We have already discussed that plastic is convenient. The problem is that plastic is *too* convenient. It is too easy to spend more than you want to or more than you realize because you are just swiping the card. You don't even have to think when you swipe your card. Just continue your conversation as you pull it out of your wallet, swipe it, put it back in your wallet, sign the sales slip and continue on your way.

But when you use cash, you actually have to stop and think about how much you are pulling out of your wallet. You have to count the money. Then you usually count the change. Both steps cause you to break your pattern, and actually pay attention to what you just did. The next time you go to buy something, your brain is more likely to remember that you already spent money since you had to count it.

Look at it another way. If you have $40 in your wallet, and you spend $15, it is easy to see that you have $25 left in your wallet. On the other hand, if you have $40 in your bank account, and you pull out your debit card, how do you know that you have $40 in your bank account? Your debit card doesn't have your current balance listed on it.

Let's assume you decide to check your account balance before you leave your room. After you have been out with your friends for a while, and made a few small purchases, your debit card still does not tell you how much your new balance is. And even if you keep your receipts and do the math, you are still treating your money like it is just a number; almost like it is make-believe. But when you have cash, it is real. And you can see that it is dwindling away.

> The problem is that plastic is *too* convenient. It is too easy to spend more than you realized or wanted to because you were just swiping the card.

What happens when you want to make a larger purchase? Do you normally carry enough cash to buy a pair of shoes? Probably not, and that is a good thing. If you are walking through the mall and see a great deal on shoes that you absolutely must have, you may buy them if you have a debit card, and are very likely to buy them if you have a credit card. But what happens if you only use cash? You will have to wait until you come back with the money. The funny thing is you are quite likely to change your mind by that time.

So does that mean you did not get your shoes? Yes, but it means you did not get shoes that were so unimportant to you anyway, that they were not worth the effort of making a second trip to the mall. Besides, if your goal was to go shopping for shoes, you would have taken enough money on that trip to buy the shoes. You would be less likely to spend money on something else; since you want to make sure you have enough for the shoes.

How much stuff do you own that you no longer use? How much of it did you stop using after just one or two times? How much did you actually never use? That is all wasted money. Using cash helps prevent you from wasting money. It is not

100% effective, but it is more effective than using plastic. One of the easiest ways to control your spending is to withdraw a certain amount of cash each week, knowing that you can only spend that amount. If you pull the money out of the bank on Friday, and see that it is almost gone by Sunday, then you know you will have to slow down your spending to get through the rest of the week.

Of course, you may want to keep your debit card on you to purchase gas for your car. If that's the case, make sure you only use it for that purpose; otherwise everything you have read so far will be wasted. Whatever you do, don't forget to account for your gas purchases when you are balancing your account. You don't want to be hit with an overdraft fee from your bank because you forgot about your pit stop.

> ## We naturally like having choices, and having cash on us gives us choices.

On a much larger scale, cash can help you save money when making certain large purchases. For instance, when you buy furniture or a car you may be offered the *choice* between 0% financing *or* cash back. Think about it. If you take the 0% financing, then you cannot take the cash back amount. If you had enough of your own money to make the purchase without the need for financing, you could take the cash back amount instead of the zero percent financing.

Remember, money gives you choices, and debt takes them away. If you are able to maintain and keep your spending under control using cash, then you are not borrowing, thus you are leaving your options open. A person who owns nothing, but has $1 in cash is worth more than someone who owns a used television worth $1,000 and has a credit card debt to go along with it for about $1,500. So owing money makes you the opposite of wealthy. It makes you poor.

Why is cash better?

_____

_____

_____

_____

How can you use cash as a way of saving more money or spending less?

_____

_____

_____

_____

Notes:

_____

_____

_____

_____

_____

_____

Thing #5

How to Keep Your Account Balanced

Chapter 10

How do I keep my account balanced?

O ne of the basic skills that nobody teaches students is how to balance a checkbook or bank account. The concept of keeping an account balanced is completely foreign to almost all students, and a large percentage of college graduates as well. There are several ways to track your account. Some are more thorough than others, but they take more time.

The easiest way to track your account balance is through internet banking, or at least accessing your account online. Since debit card purchases and ATM cash withdrawals post to your account almost instantaneously you can get a fairly accurate picture of your existing account balance. What you will not be able to see online is how many checks you have outstanding that have not yet been cashed.

For instance, if you wrote a check to your utility company and they have not yet cashed it, then your account balance will show that you have more money since your utility payment has not yet come out. Hopefully it will post within a couple of days. If you write a check to a friend, as a birthday gift or reimbursement for tickets for example, your friend may forget to cash the check for several weeks or months. When they do finally get around to cashing the check, the money will come out of your account. If you forgot about that check, then you will think that you have more money in your account than you actually do. It could really hurt if the check was for a large amount, or if your balance was very low.

Another option for maintaining your account balance is to use software. Several programs are available, including Quicken© and Microsoft© Money. With software, you can download your account statements, key in every time you write a check, and schedule your automatic withdrawals (such as car payments or student loan payments that automatically come out of your account each month). Everyone should use this software at some point for a few months just to get an idea of where you spend your money and to really understand how to track expenses. You may want to wait until after you graduate, and have more regular paychecks and regular bills before you get into something this detailed.

> **What you will not be able to see online is how many checks you have outstanding that have not yet been cashed.**

An easier option is to set up a regular spreadsheet to track your month-end bank statements and reconcile them against your actual expenses. You would also plug in any checks that you write, so you would not forget about them. If you write a check and record it on the spreadsheet, it will be easier to see if someone did not cash your check after a while. You can download a very simple spreadsheet for tracking your account balance for free at *www.ExtraCreditBook.com/excelcalcs.html*.

Keep in mind that ATM receipts are *not* the most reliable way of tracking your account balance because they are not always up to the minute accurate, and they do not account for any outstanding checks. If you do not have any outstanding checks, then you can usually look up your account online, and be relatively comfortable. It is always a safe bet to build in a cushion in your checking account. For instance, you may decide you never want your account below $50, so if you have an expense you forget about you'll be okay (as long as it is less than $50). You may want to slowly try to increase that cushion to at least $100. Just make a conscious effort each time you get paid to increase your mental cushion by another $5 or $10.

> ATM receipts are not the most reliable way of tracking your account balance because they are not always up to the minute accurate, and they do not account for any outstanding checks.

The other thing you will have to consider is cash flow. If you take on a car payment, or you are paying rent or utilities, or some other regular payment while in college, you need to plan for automatic withdrawals. If your cell phone bill automatically gets deducted on the 5th of each month, then you need to make sure you have enough in your account to cover that payment. More importantly, you need to make sure you have enough in your account on the 5th.

If you get paid every two weeks, and your last paycheck was on the 24th of the previous month, and you don't get paid again until the 7th of the next month, you have to plan for your cell phone bill which will come out *before* your next check. This is a tough situation, because you are close to the end of your two week period, so you may be close to running out of money.

As you can see, this is an example of why debt is stressful. It is bad enough when you have regular payments for things such as utilities, but when you add car payments, credit card payments and student loan payments to the mix, it can be tough since you constantly have to ensure you have enough in your account to pay each of these bills. It is also difficult when you see $1,000 sitting in your account, but you cannot spend it because that will just barely cover your rent, car insurance, utilities, cable, car payment, credit cards, and student loans. Somehow you will have to buy gas and food as well.

> **Don't forget to consider cash flow.**
> **It is important to know when your money will be**
> **deposited as well as how much.**

Each month you will receive a statement from your bank, or you can access it online. Periodically, you should check your expenses against what you actually spent (or thought you did) to make sure nobody overcharged you, and more importantly to make sure there are no unauthorized charges (a potential sign of identity theft). If there are charges for a gas station in Wyoming, and you have never been to Wyoming, then you should call the number on the back of your debit card and report the charges immediately.

If you are tracking your expenses on a spreadsheet or using the software, you should compare your transactions with your bank statement. Mark each transaction on your spreadsheet as you find the corresponding transaction on your bank statement. This way you will know which transactions you missed on your spreadsheet, which ones are still outstanding, and if any charges are for amounts different than what you recorded.

What are some ways to track your account balance?

_____

_____

_____

_____

Why is it important to maintain your account balance or not spend more than you have?

_____

_____

_____

_____

Notes:

_____

_____

_____

_____

_____

_____

_____

Thing #6

How to Understand Your Student Loans

Chapter 11

How do my student loans work?

Before you even arrive on a college campus to begin taking courses you should already have completed the Free Application for Federal Student Aid (FAFSA) process at www.fafsa.ed.gov. In order to receive nearly any type of financial aid, including scholarships, loans, grants, or even a college work-study job, you need to submit a FAFSA either electronically or by mail. The FAFSA is not just for your freshman year in college, it must be completed each year for any type of financial aid. Pay careful attention to deadlines and allow a couple of months extra time to give you a cushion for any corrections.

Before you borrow, always take advantage of any "free" money you can get. Scholarships and grants don't have to be paid back, loans do.

Student loans come in a variety of forms. The two major categories of student loans are federal student loans and private student loans. The key difference is that private student loans are provided by banks and loan companies that are not part of the federal student loan program. Private loans do not have the federally-subsidized low interest rates or any of the other defined benefits provided by the federal government.

Federal Student Loans

Federal student loans have borrowing limits, but come with a fixed interest rate. They may not require any payments to be made until six months or more after graduation. Other benefits may exist as well, such as graduated payments, hardship deferment, income-based repayment and, in some cases, loan forgiveness. In addition, most federal loans, such as the Stafford loan for undergraduate college students, do not require credit checks.

Federal student loans can be either *subsidized* or *unsubsidized*. Subsidized student loans do not accrue interest while you are in college because the government is paying the interest for you. They are based on your financial need, which is calculated from the information you report on your FAFSA. Unsubsidized loans accrue interest while you are in college, which means you will owe more when you graduate than the amount you initially borrowed. Both types of loans normally allow you to wait until six months after graduation to start making payments, but keep in mind the interest on the unsubsidized loans during those six months will be added (capitalized) to the total amount you originally borrowed.

> **Borrow all federal money first before you even consider private loans.**

Private Student Loans

Private student loans are basically unsecured loans provided by banks. They are similar to a personal loan, but are earmarked for education expenses. Otherwise, they are similar to any other bank loan. You will be required to make a monthly payment for a certain number of years. Private loans may allow you to borrow more than a federal student loan, but will usually have higher interest rates than federal student loans, and often have variable interest rates (meaning your interest rate could go up). You may also be required to undergo a credit check and possibly have a cosigner such as a parent, grandparent, or other responsible adult who has good credit.

Since private loans can vary widely and don't have as many borrower-friendly features as federal loans, you need to shop around. Just because you see a certain private loan advertised more does not make it better for you. Interest rates differ from one lender to another. A one percent difference in interest rates on $20,000 in student loans could easily cost you more than $1,000 in extra interest. Be sure to read the fine print on any private loan you are considering.

> Bankruptcy cannot eliminate
> your student loan debts.

Paying for Your Student Loans

When you take out a normal loan, such as a car loan, you immediately start making payments each month until you finally pay off the loan. Each month a portion of your payment goes towards the interest (the 'fee' you pay to borrow the bank's money) and the rest goes towards the principal (the total amount that you still owe). Student loans work almost the same way, but with a slightly different twist.

With federal student loans you do not have to make your monthly payment while you are in college. In fact, you don't have to start making payments until six months or more after you leave school. This "grace period" gives you a chance to find a job, get adjusted, etc. However, your total loan amount at graduation will depend on the type of loan you had while in college. There are three basic types of loans and each one treats interest differently. In the following scenario we will assume you borrowed $1,000 each year of college, interest rates are 6% for federal loans, and 8% for private loans and you graduated on time after four years. Since the average, full-time undergraduate borrows closer to $8,000 per year, we will look at those numbers as well:

For a *subsidized* federal loan, the government will pay the 6% interest for you while you are in college and during your grace period. In our example, your loan balance will be exactly $4,000 when you graduate and begin making payments after a six-month grace period. If you borrow $8,000 per year, you would owe $32,000 by the time you graduate in four years and start making payments after a six-month grace period.

> The average undergraduate leaves college with $24,000 in debt—that's $276 a month out of every paycheck for 10 years.

For an *unsubsidized* federal loan, even though you only borrowed $4,000 during your four years, you are responsible for the 6% interest from the day you borrowed the loan. The government does not pay the interest for you. The interest accumulates during your four years of college and during the grace period. Even though you only borrowed $4,000, the same as the subsidized borrower, you will owe $4,720 when you start making payments after a six-month grace period. That is because for each $1,000 you borrowed you owe $60 interest every year and during the grace period. Because of the interest that's accumulating, your payments on a standard 10-year repayment plan will be 18% higher each month (or $8.00 higher in this example). If you borrow $8,000 per year, you would owe more than $37,760 ($32,000 plus $5,760 in interest) by the time you graduate in four years and start making payments after a six-month grace period! This means your monthly payment would be $64.00 higher than the subsidized federal loan.

For a *private* loan, you will have to read the fine print to see how the lender treats your interest while you are in college and during your grace period, if there is one. While some private loans treat your interest the same as federal unsubsidized loans, the lender can compound your interest charges while you are in school. Not only does interest accumulate during your four years of college and your grace period, you also pay interest on the interest! That means even though you only borrowed a total of $4,000 at 8%, you will owe $5,081 when you start making payments after a six-month grace period (if the private lender offers a grace period). If you borrow $8,000 per year, you would owe more than $40,646 ($32,000 plus $8,646 in interest) by the time you graduate in four years and start making payments! This means your monthly payment would be $138.00 higher than the subsidized federal loan or $74.00 more than the unsubsidized federal loan.

> ### Student loans must be repaid
> ### even if you drop out of college!

Smart Borrowing

Students who borrow a federal student loan for the first time are required to go through entrance loan counseling. The purpose is to help you understand your loan responsibilities, and it should give you some tips and tools for managing your student loan borrowing. Even if you've borrowed before, it's a good idea to go through this counseling session. Often, you can complete it online and take a required quiz. If your school has the resources, try to speak directly with someone at your school who can explain everything to you one-on-one. The counseling session explains your rights, your responsibilities, the interest costs, your repayment options, and more. Pay attention to the information, because borrowing a student loan will affect your finances for several years after you graduate or leave school.

It is important that you understand the consequences of borrowing money for college. Now is the time to take control of what your future payments will be. It's impossible to make adjustments in how much you've borrowed if you wait until graduation. Pay attention to how much you are borrowing and, more importantly, how much of your future income you'll be devoting to your student loan payments.

> Keep an eye on your student loan amounts while you are still in school. You don't want a big "shocker" after graduation.

The best approach is to carefully keep track of what you borrow, and periodically look at the total amount you already owe *before* you borrow again. At the beginning of each school year, ask the financial aid office for a list of all your loans and what your total monthly payment will be. You can also review your federal student loans online at _www.nslds.ed.gov_. Understanding how much your loans cost will help you control your borrowing and ask only for what you absolutely need.

One of the biggest mistakes I see college students making is spending their entire student loan during the first few weeks of the semester. It is difficult for anyone, much less a college freshman, to suddenly have a large amount of money in the bank and to keep it from affecting their spending habits. After all, if you have $3,000 in your account at the beginning of the semester, $20 for a few movie tickets, $5 for an energy smoothie, or even $5 for an overpriced notebook at the bookstore may seem like reasonable expenses. Each purchase is just a drop in the bucket compared to $3,000. Instead, you need to look at your student loan money as just $500 per month for the next six months. When you compare each purchase to a $500 account balance it will seem like a bigger deal.

In addition, think about what you are doing when you make purchases with your student loan money. Since most student loans are paid off over 10 years or more, you are essentially paying for your purchases with interest charges that you'll be paying for 10 years after you graduate. So, you do not want to spend borrowed money on a cell phone which you will likely trade off after just two years, or buy a coffee that will be gone before your first class begins, or purchase lunch that will only last a half hour. In other words, avoid using your student loan money to pay for things that only last a short period of time because you will still be paying for it for many years after you graduate.

> If you borrow just $250 extra each year
> for four years at 6% you will end up
> working an extra 120 hours after graduation
> to pay it back if you make $36,000 per year.

If you realize you have borrowed more than you need, you can always choose to cancel the loan or return the extra. You will owe less, have smaller monthly payments and pay less interest in the long-run.

You also have the option to make regular payments while you're in college to avoid having a large chunk of interest added on to your student loan. If you can afford to make these payments, it will save you money in the long-run. But your first priority should be making payments on credit cards and other high-cost loans. If you do not have any other debt and you are able to make payments on your college loans, they should be your next priority.

Managing Your Loan Payments

With most student loans you are given a 6-month grace period after you leave school before you must start making payments. You can choose to make payments right away, or wait until the grace period expires and you receive a bill from your lender. The standard repayment on most student loans is ten years. Your monthly payment amount is determined by the interest rate, the amount you borrow, and the number of years it will take to pay off the loan. The more you owe, the higher your monthly payment. The higher your interest rate, the higher your monthly payment. The longer you take to pay off your loan, the lower your monthly payment, but you will pay more interest and use more of your monthly income over a longer period to make your payments.

> Once you graduate, you are usually given a
> 6-month grace period before you have to
> start making payments on federal student loans.

There are many different repayment plans on federal student loans. For example, if you cannot afford to pay rent and make your student loan payment, you may want graduated payments. They start smaller than what your regular monthly payment should be, then gradually get larger every few years until the loan is paid off. The theory is that students start out making entry-level salaries, but will gradually increase their salaries as they gain more experience. Another option might be an income-based repayment (IBR) plan, which is available if your federal student loan debt is high relative to your income and family size. Your payments will be lower with IBR, but you may pay a lot more in interest over time because your loan could last up to 25 years. You also have to provide proof of your income and family size each year.

Your lender will explain your loan repayment options. If you borrowed a federal loan, your college's financial aid office provides exit loan counseling when you graduate. They will discuss your loan amounts, repayment options and other obligations at this meeting. Be sure to ask any questions you may have at this time.

> You will never find a more borrower-friendly loan than a student loan because there are so many repayment options. Contact your lender if you are having financial difficulty.

In some instances, your federal student loans can be forgiven or repaid for you if you choose certain careers or occupations, such as teaching, primary care physician, or public service work. The purpose of these programs is to entice individuals to work in a particular job or high-need area for a number of years. Some employers, including the federal government, offer loan repayment plans in exchange for working for a specified number of years.

This is a serious benefit to consider if you are fortunate enough to have multiple job offers. However, you should not make the loan forgiveness or repayment benefit the primary reason for choosing a particular employer, job or career. There are specific requirements you'll have to meet and not all employers and not all federal government jobs offer these benefits. So you will have to research each job offer and consider all the options to decide if the commitment you'll be making is worth the benefit you'll receive.

If all of the above payment options still result in payments that are more than you can afford, you can also apply for deferred payments. This is a short-term fix and is best used when you have not yet found a full-time position. Deferred payments will buy you some time, but if your job simply pays too little to afford the minimum payments this option will not do you much good.

Keep in mind that your interest continues to accrue while in deferment (unless the loan is subsidized), which means you will owe more when you finally begin making payments.

You should contact your lender to discuss your loan options if you have any difficulty making your payments.

Which type of student loan does not charge interest to you while you are still in college?

_____

_____

_____

_____

How can you minimize the amount of money you owe on student loans?

_____

_____

_____

_____

Notes:

_____

_____

_____

_____

_____

_____

Thing #7

How to Avoid Identity Theft

Chapter 12

What is identity theft?

Identity theft is one of the fastest growing crimes in our country and in the world. The consequences of identity theft can actually haunt you for many years, and maybe even the rest of your life. Sometimes students think they are not vulnerable because they do not have a credit history yet or they do not have enough money to worry about it.

The problem is that identity theft is much more significant than just losing a credit card. A person can use your information to get a license, title their car in your name, and much more. Think about it; do you really want someone else living as you? of course not! They will be living a life much nicer than the one you have since they get to play with money that is not theirs. Plus they do not have to repay it… you do!

The problem is that in many ways you may be more vulnerable *because* you are a student. You are very mobile and you are unlikely to be checking your credit report regularly. That means criminals may get to use your identity for a long time before you even have any idea what is happening. Fortunately there are several things you can do to prevent identity theft.

1. Do not leave your cards laying around

Make sure you do not leave your credit or debit cards lying around. Definitely do not leave anything with your social security number lying around either. Even if you perfectly trust your roommate, think about the number of "friends" they may bring into your room/apartment. If you leave your cards or identifying information lying on the front seat of your car, smart criminals (which is almost an oxymoron) may see the opportunity and break into your car and steal your information.

2. Never share your PIN

Never share your ATM/debit card PIN. In fact you really should never share any PIN or password with anyone. Again, you may trust your roommate, but nobody is perfect. I am not trying to make you paranoid, just cautious. Once someone has your PIN, they can more easily get access to your money, especially if they are able to also write down your card number, or if they swipe it early one morning while you are still in bed. Do not trust access to your money to anyone.

3. Shred the important stuff

Do not recycle or throw away anything with your personal information on it in the regular trash. You can always tear off the portion that has your information and recycle the rest. Credit card statements, bank statements, and receipts that have credit card, social security, address or any other personal information on it should be shredded and disposed of properly. For fun, I like to scoop the cat litter and dump in with my shredded documents so if someone really wants to try and dig through my trash and piece together my information, they really have to go through a lot of crap... literally.

4. Do not carry your social security card with you

Do not carry your social security card in your wallet and avoid using your social security number if you can. If someone steals your wallet and gets your social security number, driver's license (with your address), your credit card numbers and more, then they can do almost anything they want with your identity at that point. Keep your social security card somewhere else besides your wallet. When someone asks for your social security number (such as a doctor's office, etc.) ask them if you can use some other form of identification instead. Sometimes they will comply, sometimes they have no choice.

5. Be very careful online

Fake links and fake emails can lure you into providing confidential information. Never email personal information such as credit card numbers or your social security number. Email is not secure. In fact, never enter your social security number or credit card information online unless your browser indicates you are on a secure site. In the case of your social security number you better really trust that site, such as one from a major bank, your college, etc.

Okay, so what happens if something happens to your identity even if it is not your fault?

1) First, contact the TransUnion Fraud Assistance Department at (800-680-7289) and report the incident.

2) Then you should contact your credit card companies to let them know your identity may have been stolen.

3) Next, you will need to file a police report.

4) Finally, you will need to contact the Federal Trade Commission which has an ID theft affidavit to fill out and send to your creditors.

That will not end your ordeal with identity theft; it is only the beginning, but the earlier you get the process started, the less damage that will occur.

If only a credit card or debit card gets stolen or lost and not all of your other information, then just call the issuer of your card or cards. Follow their guidance, but if purchases were made on your cards, you may wish to file a police report. If no purchases were made, you will not be held responsible for any attempted purchases after you report the card stolen.

To avoid scams, remember that anytime someone solicits you and needs a decision "Right away," the decision should be "No thanks." You need time to think before reacting to make a decision.

Also, keep in mind the basics of economics and investments, which is the balance between risk and reward. If someone has an opportunity for you to double your money in six weeks, it is either a scam or it is extremely risky (almost as risky as betting your money in Vegas). If they say they can *guarantee* to double your money, then it is a scam. The greater the possible return on your money, the greater the risk of losing it all.

If anyone calls you to report a problem with your account and asks to verify your information, don't do it. Remember, you will never give your credit card information out unless you initiate the phone call. Call the number on the back of your credit card to verify, ask questions, or report problems. Never trust anyone who calls you and asks for information.

The point is that it takes just a little effort to prevent identity theft, but a lot of effort to fix it once it happens to you.

What steps can you take to protect your personal identity?

_____

_____

_____

_____

How can you identify a scam?

_____

_____

_____

_____

Notes:

_____

_____

_____

_____

_____

_____

_____

BONUS Thing

How to Succeed in College

Chapter 13

Get involved
on your campus

One of the leading causes of students dropping out of college, after financial issues and academic failure, is poor social fit. Students that choose not to get involved in campus organizations and activities, and especially those who go "home" every weekend, tend to be the ones who are unable to succeed at school. One of the advantages of going to college is the huge social network. Your mood will improve, your life will improve, and ultimately you will find yourself more successful.

I felt miserable my first year of college, but once I got involved and joined the student government association, my entire outlook on college improved. You have so many options to choose from. There are organizations for almost every belief, goal, or cause. I read a quote that said, "If you stand for nothing, then you will fall for anything." Join an organization or a cause and become involved.

There are four primary reasons to join organizations on your campus, or even in your community. 1) Explore social interests. 2) Meet new people. 3) Develop skills to include on your resume. 4) Have fun. All four are excellent reasons to get involved and they will also result in improving your life.

Explore social interests

Are you absolutely certain what you want to do with the rest of your life? By exploring your social interests not only will you have an outlet after class, but you may also learn more about yourself in the process. Perhaps you will find a way to match what you love doing with your career choice.

Meet new people

In the business world we call this networking. You will make new friends, interact with faculty and advisors, and meet others who may currently work in your field of interest. Your interactions with the business community as well as your campus community could lead to long lasting friendships as well as future business or job opportunities.

Develop skills to include on your resume

In high school, most organizations were run by teachers with students as passive participants. In college, most organizations are actually run by the students with little involvement by the faculty. That means by joining an organization you immediately begin to develop the kind of skills that employers are seeking.

A leadership position allows you to gain all types of experience, such as organizing a fundraiser or an event, scheduling travel, or attending conferences. Most organizations have some type of budget so you can reference that on your resume (such as, "allocated $12,000 annually in activity funds for our organization.")

Just participating in a group will usually result in contributing in some way to a successful community service event. Whether you help raise awareness for the plight of two-headed turtles or help organize a showing of a foreign film, you are demonstrating useful skills that employers will want to hear about in your resume.

Have fun

There is nothing wrong with having fun. A positive attitude could mean the difference between success and failure in some of your classes. You will never again have so many different types of opportunities available to you to do so many things than while you are in college. So go ahead and join an organization or activity just to have some fun. You will be surprised where that could lead you.

30% of college and university students drop out after their first year. Half never graduate.

Studies indicate that students who get involved on campus enjoy college more, are more likely to graduate on time, and find it easier to seek jobs. Your involvement could lead to better time management and interpersonal skills which are critical to your success in an interview and for career advancement.

Even if you commute to class or attend a two-year institution it is critical that you get involved. If not, you will not only miss out on the obvious career benefits, but you will also miss out on a large portion of what college has to offer. It may be difficult to divide your time among class, work, family life, and other activities, but find the right balance and it just doesn't get any better. Keep in mind to have fun along the way. In college it really is about the journey and not just the destination.

Why are you less likely to succeed in college if you do not become involved in some type of organization or activity?

_____

_____

_____

_____

What are some ways you can become involved on your campus?

_____

_____

_____

_____

Notes:

_____

_____

_____

_____

_____

_____

_____

Chapter 14

Do I need
an internship?

When you graduate, there will be almost 1.8 million people just like you. In order to compete in the job market you need to get an interview. Your resume, transcript, and work experience will be the top three factors that determine whether or not you get that interview.

To create the best resume possible you should get assistance from your career center on your campus early in your college career and again when you are about to graduate.

Since your potential employer wants to know how well you did in certain classes pertaining to your career path they may request your transcript. It is up to you to take the right classes and do well in them during your next few years. It may only take a 'D' to pass a class but most employers will not look too kindly on someone who only does just enough to get by.

An internship is something that you can start to work on at any point while you are in college with the emphasis on, "while you are in college." Work with your career services office or academic department and seek opportunities to get an internship.

Did you know that more than 80% of companies surveyed said they use internships as recruiting tools? In addition, and you really want to pay attention to this… more than three quarters of the companies surveyed said they prefer candidates with the kind of relevant work experience gained through an internship. If you are looking for a sign, there it is.

If you know someone who already graduated but has been unable to find a job, I will bet they did not complete an internship prior to graduation. Of course an internship is not a total guarantee of employment, but if you want to play the numbers so to speak, get an internship. Otherwise you will be competing against those who do, leaving you just a very small sliver of jobs to choose from.

What am I talking about? According to a survey by The National Association of Colleges and Employers, almost half of the companies' new graduate hires came from their own internship programs. That means almost one out of every two jobs for college graduates is already going to be taken by someone who interned with that company. So if you are not interning for the company you want to work for, you may have lost out on half of the job opportunities. That means if you cannot get an internship with the company you want to work for, then at least get an internship somewhere.

> You will be competing with more than 2 million other people just like you when you graduate.

If you are not convinced that you will need some type of internship before graduation, then practice these six words… you'll need them soon enough. "Would you like fries with that?"

Seriously, when it comes to competing you want to bring something to the table. The inability to get an internship is not a career death sentence, but it will be that much more difficult to get hired. There are other options as well, including holding leadership positions for organizations on campus and so forth. A leadership position is not just a president, but it also includes the chairperson of any particular event, cause, or fundraiser. The key is to be in charge of something and make it a success.

So how can you find an internship? You should visit the career services office. No, it is not just for people that are six weeks from graduation. Why do you think it is open all semester long? You can also consult your specific academic department or advisor for suggestions. Many job sites also have resources online by using the keyword "intern".

Of course, there are plenty of students looking for these limited opportunities, so keep in mind you are just one small fish competing with millions of other small fish. Your best approach is to use your connections on and off campus. Talk to your instructors, your department chairs and anyone you know from the industry or who knows someone in the industry. Basically ask anyone who will listen. Use your social network sites, your parents, your friends' parents or your parents' friends. Most great opportunities do not come by chance; they come through your connections. When it comes to jobs, it really is less about what you know and more about who you know.

> An internship will give you a
> competitive edge when you graduate.

You can also talk to companies face-to-face. Go to career fairs and look for internship opportunities. I often give my students extra credit for attending career fairs. I am not surprised that each semester at least a handful of those who are not seniors come back and tell me they got one or more internship opportunities. See, sometimes your professors really do have your best interests in mind. Some other opportunities to find internships include going directly to individual company websites as well as intern specific websites such as *InternJobs.com, InternWeb.com,* or *GetThatGig.com.*

Some key advice. Do not pass up an internship just because it does not pay. It is the experience, not the salary that will make the difference in your life. Sure, you'll miss a few movies and concerts during the semester, but it is a small sacrifice to make when your internship lands you a job that keeps you from moving back home with your parents after graduation.

Nothing says congratulations graduate like having your mom fold your underwear... or worse yet, your dad (right, ladies?). A few dollars today means very little in the grand scheme of things. Again, it goes back to why are you here in college? What is your goal? You want to gain skills that will entice employers to hire you... at unheard of salaries.

> **With internships, it is the experience, not the salary that will make the difference in your life.**

Now, just getting an internship will not secure a job for you. It is another tool to help you reach your goal. So how can you get the most out of your internship? You need to use the networking opportunity. Build professional relationships. Try to avoid just doing grunt work... stuff that a high school intern could do. You want to work on projects with people. Find a mentor. Listen to their advice and find out what they did right and what they did wrong on their way up the corporate ladder.

You need to think of your internship as a 6-week or 15-week interview process. Be professional, dress professionally, never show up late, and always show a positive attitude. Avoid office gossip or negativity. If you are not given the right types of opportunities, then take some initiative. You want them to like your work and remember you since they may be your key reference for the next couple of jobs.

Keep in mind, an internship is more than just a checkmark on your to-do list like some of your required courses. You want to gain experiences. The kind of experiences that will allow you to have smart, thorough and substantive answers to questions during your job interviews after graduation. That means you have to be your own best advocate for your career.

Why should you get an internship while you are in college?

_____

_____

_____

_____

How can you get the most out of an internship?

_____

_____

_____

_____

Notes:

_____

_____

_____

_____

_____

_____

Web Resources

www.ExtraCreditBook.com
The Website for this book!

www.TheGraduatesGuide.com
One of Bill's other websites for college graduates

www.BillPrattSeminars.com
Another of Bill's websites

www.YoungMoney.com
A good site full of money and career advice for students and recent graduates

Books (Recommended Reading)

The Graduate's Guide to Life & Money/2E, Bill Pratt (2011)

Graduation Debt: How to Manage Student Loans and Live Your Life, Reyna Gobel (2010)

Out on My Own... Now What?, Joe Kahler (2005)

Financial Peace Revisited, Dave Ramsey (2003)

The Millionaire Next Door, Thomas J. Stanley and William D. Danko (1998)

Sources

Chapter 1 – Statistic: 38% of students who drop out of school do so because of debt/financial pressure, making it the number one reason, compared to academic failure reported by 28% of students dropping out. Source: Deep Underground Credit Knowledge 9. *http://www.duck9.com/College-Student-Drop-Out-Rates.htm*. Accessed 1/2/10.

Chapter 2 – Information: What makes up a credit score? Source: What's in your FICO® score. MyFico.com. *http://www.myfico.com/CreditEducation/WhatsInYourScore.aspx*. Accessed 6/20/2010.

Information: Cost of a credit score. Sources: *www.MyFico.com*, *www.experian.com*.

Chapter 3 – Statistic: The average college graduate overestimates his or her starting salary by 44%. Source: Big Loans, Bigger Problems: A Report on the Sticker Shock of Student Loans, March 2001 (Tracey King and Ivan Frishberg); *www.pirg.org*.

Statistic: If you use credit cards instead of cash you will spend 12-18% more. Source: *http://www.daveramsey.com/the_truth_about/credit_card_debt_3478.html.cfm*. Accessed 5/12/08.

Chapter 7 – Statistic: Americans spend over $580 billion annually dining out. Source: National Restaurant Association; "Restaurant Industry Outlook Brightens in 2010 as Sales, Economy Are Expected to Improve." January 20, 2010.

Chapter 8 – Statistic: 71% of Americans age 18-24 use a debit card in any given month. Source: Creditcards.com; *http://www.creditcards.com/credit-card-news/credit-card-industry-facts-personal-debt-statistics-1276.php#ixzz1A1wLfkjz*. Accessed 1/3/2010.

Statistic: 74% of monthly college spending is with cash and debit cards. Only 7 percent is with credit cards. Source: Creditcards.com. *http://www.creditcards.com/credit-card-news/credit-card-industry-facts-personal-debt-statistics-1276.php#ixzz1A1wqQdu2*. Accessed 1/3/2010.

Chapter 11 – Information about student loans (various). Source: *www.inceptia.org*. Contributions from Inceptia staff.

Statistic: The average undergraduate leaves college with $24,000 in debt. Source: 2003-04 National Postsecondary Student Aid Study (NPSAS:04); National Center for Education Statistics (published June 2005).

Statistic: The average, full-time undergraduate borrows $8,000 per year.
Source: 2003-04 National Postsecondary Student Aid Study (NPSAS:04);
National Center for Education Statistics (published June 2005).

Chapter 13 – Statistic: Thirty percent of college and university students drop out after their first year. Half never graduate. Source: Bowler, Mike. *Dropouts Loom Large for Schools*. U.S. News. August 9, 2009. Accessed 1/3/2010. *http://www.usnews.com/education/best-colleges/articles/2009/08/19/dropouts-loom-large-for-schools.htm*.

Information: Studies indicate that students who get involved on campus enjoy college more… Sources:
http://www.uwp.edu/departments/residence.life/involvement.cfm
http://www.fullerton.edu/deanofstudents/getinvolved/index.html

Chapter 14 – Statistic: More than 80% of companies surveyed said they use internships as recruiting tools. Source: Internship Programs Feed Full-Time Hiring. NACE. *http://www.naceweb.org/Publications/Spotlight_Online/2010/0428/Internship_Programs_Feed_Full-Time_Hiring.aspx*. Accessed 6/19/2010.

Statistic: More than three quarters of the companies surveyed… gained through an internship. Source: Internship Experience Key to Employment for New College Grads. NACE. h*ttp://www.naceweb.org/Press/Releases/Internship_Experience_Key_to_Employment_for_New_College_Grads_(12-11-09).aspx*. Accessed 6/19/2010.

Statistic: Almost half of the companies' new graduate hires came from their own internship programs. Source: Internship Could Be Step to First Job. NACE. *http://www.naceweb.org/Publications/Spotlight_Online/2010/0512/Internship_Could_Be_Step_to_First_Job.aspx*. Accessed 6/19/2010.

Statistic: More than 2 million graduates. Source: Digest of Education Statistics; National Center for Education Statistics. Table 247.

Trademarks

Barbie™ is a trademark of Mattel, Inc.
Monopoly™ is a trademark of Hasbro.
eBay® is a registered trademark of eBay®.

Need More Extra Credit?

Extra Credit: The 7 Things Every College Student Needs to Know about Credit, Debt & Ca$h is available at quantity discounts for bulk purchases. Visit *www.inceptia.org/books* for information.

Also available from Bill Pratt

The Graduate's Guide to Life and Money
Finally, a book designed for recent college graduates that helps them deal with their unique circumstances and challenges with life and money. It includes everything from getting a job, finding an apartment, getting out of debt to getting married! This is a must-have book for the soon-to-be graduate or for anyone under the age of thirty who is not currently independently wealthy.

Visit *www.inceptia.org/books* for ordering information. Quantity discounts are available for bulk purchases.

Bill Pratt is available to speak at your school, company, organization, or association event.

Bill Pratt
740 Greenville Blvd. Ste. 400, #165
Greenville, NC 27858
301-788-2711
info@ViaticusGroup.com
www.BillPrattSeminars.com

Bill Pratt

B ill Pratt is the author of several books on personal finance including *The Graduate's Guide to Life and Money*, *How to Keep Your Kid from Moving Back Home after College* (June 2012), and a textbook on personal finance. His books help students and young adults improve their finances and their lives.

Bill is a former economist for the federal government and a former vice president for Citigroup. He left the financial industry to focus his efforts on helping others understand money.

Bill is Vice President of Viaticus, a financial education company. He is a college instructor at East Carolina University in Greenville, North Carolina, and Assistant Director of the ECU College of Business Financial Wellness Initiative. He also speaks professionally to college students and adults on topics ranging from money to careers. He holds an MBA in finance.

Bill's goal is to help students wade through the endless financial and life decisions they will encounter. By making the best decisions about life and money with the right attitude, Bill believes that people will accumulate more wealth faster and will then be able to use that wealth to improve the lives of those around them.

About Inceptia

Inceptia, a leading provider of financial success tools for young adults, is proud to collaborate with our colleague Bill Pratt, to bring you this useful guide to financial management. Inceptia believes strongly, that if applied, the principles in this book will help you lead an enriched financial life.

Together with esteemed author and financial expert Bill Pratt, Inceptia presents personal financial management seminars on campuses throughout the country. Inceptia's online financial education program teaches young adults the basics of financial management in an engaging environment. Inceptia is a passionate advocate for ensuring young adults of all backgrounds have access to the information, tools, and resources needed to understand their financial rights and responsibilities so that they can make informed financial decisions today and throughout their lives.

To learn more about how Inceptia can help you launch brilliant futures, call 888-529-2028 or visit *www.inceptia.org.*

Additional Notes